Red Haws to Light the Field

ESSENTIAL POETS SERIES 243

Canada

Guernica Editions Inc. acknowledges the support of the Canada Council for the Arts and the Ontario Arts Council. The Ontario Arts Council is an agency of the Government of Ontario.

We acknowledge the financial support of the Government of Canada.

Red Haws to Light the Field

James Deahl

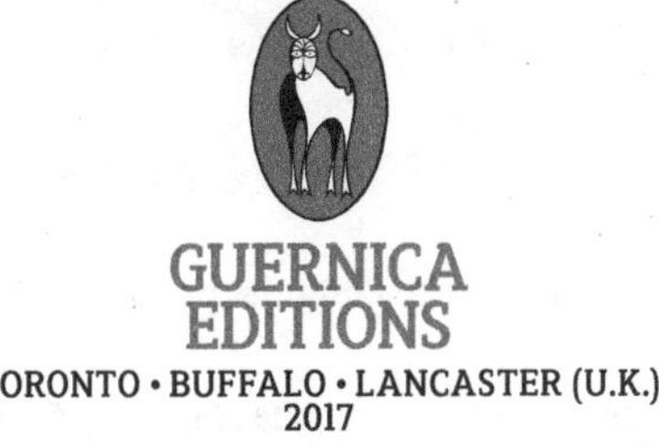

GUERNICA EDITIONS
TORONTO • BUFFALO • LANCASTER (U.K.)
2017

Michael Mirolla, editor
David Moratto, cover and interior design
Guernica Editions Inc.
1569 Heritage Way, Oakville, (ON), Canada L6M 2Z7
2250 Military Road, Tonawanda, N.Y. 14150-6000 U.S.A.
www.guernicaeditions.com

Distributors:
University of Toronto Press Distribution,
5201 Dufferin Street, Toronto (ON), Canada M3H 5T8
Gazelle Book Services, White Cross Mills
High Town, Lancaster LA1 4XS U.K.

First edition.
Printed in Canada.

Legal Deposit—Third Quarter
Library of Congress Catalog Card Number: 2016952734
Library and Archives Canada Cataloguing in Publication
Deahl, James, 1945-, author
Red haws to light the field / James Deahl. -- First edition.

(Essential poets series ; 243)
Poems.
ISBN 978-1-77183-198-7 (paperback)

I. Title. II. Series: Essential poets series ; 243

PS8557.A24M53 2017 C811'.54 C2016-905970-7

Dedicated with enduring love
to
Gilda L. Mekler
(1954–2007)
these final poems she helped me complete

&

Rebekah Daniell
our granddaughter

Contents

1. Where Rapture Embraces All

2. Calling The Throat To Sing

5. Nobody But You

6. A Rain of Grief

7. From Roses of Death

1

Where Rapture Embraces All

Breakfast On The Road

Although spring is close
winter has soaked into the land
and is too stubborn to leave.
A silver sky holds the memory
of snow. The diner windows
are ghosted with steam,
every tune on the juke box
at least twenty-five years old.
Why worry about my poverty?
I eat homefries and sausage
in the redbrick morning,
lay plans to visit Hartford later.

The abandoned canal reminds
of more prosperous times;
some of these buildings must go back
to early mercantile days, to what
we want to imagine was a period
of innocence, and long for again.
I sit drinking a second coffee
in Plainville, Connecticut
while listening to Ray Charles,
mechanics from the service station
two booths away, when the sun
breaks through like luck.

Dundurn

They held cockfights not far from the manor house.
The octagonal building still stands, elegant and noble,
but the birds have been gone for over a century.
Fortunes were won and lost, weapons drawn;
no one remembers what secrets the harbour holds.

This afternoon it's Chinese exercise. This is the year
of the rooster. A dozen men and women turn
in slow motion, their every pose delicate,
their loose clothing catching the breeze; each step
impeccable, like a heron hunting bass.
Now the city intends to raze the pavilion where
the Highlanders would perform in the summer heat,
their music pure as heather.

The gentleman with the silk waistcoat
and military bearing, the one Virginia said
possessed the slim fingers of a pianist, wheels
and walks toward the shore. A boat is waiting.
It rocks to the motion of water as gulls cry.

Wychwood Park

after a painting by Mary Hiester Reid

Near dusk a November sky
dips its hands into the pond.
Nightbirds hide among pale reeds;
the first parlour lights switch on.

The silence of the world surrounds you
as your shadow stands in water.
Ripples move, spread, relapse.
Night is the only philosopher—

your living blood the only warmth
as air and earth embrace.

Modigliani's Door

You sit in a chair in your studio,
the grey of April in Paris
filling the Seine with ghosts.
There was, of course, the war,
but that seemed hardly to matter
when there was pigment and blank canvas.
Years later, every frustrated drawing,
balled into your fist and tossed out,
would be pressed flat for the museum.
Behind your chair stands a door,
solid wood panels with an elliptical knob
that cannot turn, an artistic device.

If Abraham cried out to Heaven today
would God answer? Would He bless
this collection of Jews in their struggle
to re-create their world? You paint red,
orange, black, peach, every colour
alive on your palette, alive in your mind,
calling forth a mouth, a background,
the dress of a woman flowing to a corner.

How is it you love the background
more than the woman posed in front?
In the chamber beyond the door:
all the true colours—the true red
of a lover's lips, the true blue of her eyes.
If you drink too much, does it matter?
Death embraces all. Her portrait lives,
but your lover takes her own life.
In the corner, an orange head emerges from
blue-grey stone. Your hand moves
across the canvas and, though you
cannot see it, the door begins to open.

Ink On Paper: Jackson Pollock, 1951

What can one man do
in this life of thorns
but strive to break free—
to surge out of bounds
like a whale breaking the surface
of the Sound to twist in air
for a single, glistening instant.

In this sequence, the woman
is lying on her side
before vanishing where the blue
of evening prefaces night.
A man works without knowing
how life will turn out,
except that all days end in night.

Only like this do journeys begin:
the map on the table, a fresh
salt breeze parting the curtains,
perhaps lust for a woman
or the oblivion of drink.
And always that blue
falling towards darkness
where all light is absorbed.

But, one may ask, where
does the woman go?
To what desire does she answer?
The only true replies are made
by the salt breeze and the cries
of gulls pillaging the Sound.

All your journeys lead
between the world of thorns
and unconscious images
of world and non-world,
cast into your mind
like tides running the shingle.
So the painter moves
from a marsh full of birds
to that endless blue
where distinction vanishes,
where rapture embraces all.

When an afternoon rain comes in
off the sea, slanting
grey among the arms of trees,
you fold up the map
and begin.

Flame Tower

The fire through the trees
is a Moorish window
hung on the wall of the night.

Inside the flame, lust flows
and is consumed
by its own burning, its own desire.

I think of Mingus playing in
the south of France,
sailing free on a hot breeze of summer.

An airless wind comes out of Africa,
a desert where the soul is lost
and found again in its blue sirocco.

Barton Street Bus

Who can refuse to live his own life?
—Harvey Shapiro

Block following block of shops—Polish,
Serbian, White Russian—some closed forever,
others about to close, on a grey day
with the mills on lay-off, once more
on lay-off. Winds congregate in church yards
where English is spoken during special
"English only" masses, they swirl a litter of leaves,
rattling locust pods against the grand, carved doors.

Barton Street in late afternoon, and there
can be no bitterness here; the windows
of a pierogi shop steam against November's cold.
It seems the days of honeyed sesame seeds
and paprika sausage will never fade.
Yet Martin's—the finest steak house
in all Hamilton—stands boarded up,
the man in formal dress no longer keeping the door.

Oh, where have they gone? The armies
of those displaced by Europe's brutalities.
They toiled for decades within
the great steelsheds by the harbour,
in the foundries that set our night ablaze.
A few still shop at the Staropolskie Delikatesy
amid the police and firemen. Fewer still
send oldest sons into the priesthood.

An east wind traces the south shore
of Lake Ontario, piles snowclouds high
over Grimsby. What a strange world
they are passing through—these Italians,
these Portuguese! Their children speaking
a foreign tongue in the difficult weather
of Canada. The bus drives deeper into autumn,
each day shorter, each life lived without regret.

Room In Brooklyn

after a painting by Edward Hopper

Dawn; still too early
for radios or cars.
The redbrick apartments
remain turned inward
with sleep.

The air off the Upper Bay
is fresh, slightly salty.
This is the hour when
a state of grace
might be imagined.

The woman is reading
The Confessions of St. Augustine,
his passage contrasting
time present with time past.
This morning, time awaits.

Only the white flowers
standing in their white vase
show us that our present
is here and only here,
four flights above the city.

2

Calling The Throat To Sing

November Sunrise

Morning opens to the rain's music
dripping from the sumac's banners.
The murderous crows are silent;
they remain on the mountain of night.
Under their blanket of leaves
insects turn darkness to bone.

To the east the sky brightens like faith
when our modern world lies distant,
its machinery stilled in this last
hour of grace; and the wind lies down
on the soaked earth to await
the arrival of winter.

This is the season when we remember
who we are, our real names awake
on our tongues. When I walk outside
I'm alone under a silver sky,
the rain's conversation
life's only song this morning.

November Nightfall

After its journey behind cloudbanks
our sun reclines in the dark house
and the only thing left to us
is this drumming of rain on shingles.
We are castaways in night's
rushing cataract of sound.

The last of the maples flame saffron
in a north wind's grip, their branches
lifting bonfire leaves into the
driving rain, for theirs is a nameless
hunger. Redemption beckons
from the dark path we follow.

My travels have always led me here
as if this were the only place.
November breathes through the woodlot.
Every driven leaf tells its story:
a history of suffering
that when night falls turns to prayer.

Night Stars Over Gage Park

Since dawn a mist
has hung in the branches
as if to drape these January trees
with winter foliage.

A grey day
of almost melting snow
the sun barely clearing the escarpment
by noon

and in the park
only the odd retriever
and its master take paths where autumn
once held sway.

For only this
season of lean days
lays bare a harsher beauty, less ornate
than October's glow

or April's green
exuberance.
In winter every unfleshed bone reveals
life's patterns.

It is now
during my shortened days
that I begin to perceive how stars
convey meaning;

how the night sky
is a brilliant text by which
intention is understood as more than matter,
form, and energy.

And behind the trees
Jupiter climbs white in the east
like a sea rising to a lighthoused shore
to speak of

a vast creation,
a tide of light
that leafless trees strive vivid against,
each bough alive.

Old Song

The black cherry came down
last night
heartwood eaten by insects.

In my bones a shudder
a mountain stream tumbling over
a sudden cliff

its pain
calling the throat
to sing.

The Jack Pine

In memoriam: Tom Thomson (1877–1917)

Always a lake.
Always the rock
bare and severe.
Always a renegade pine
shaped to wind and storm.
This, then, is our station,
our emblem
and point of pilgrimage.
Here on this jut of earth
we begin and end,
like any year, its cycle
starting and finishing
on that shortest day of all.

The time is spring,
the green on the hills
no longer solely supplied
by pine and spruce.
But the lake water retains
the slate of winter,
that cast-iron surface
dull as a hammer blow.
The Jack pine, fireborn
years ago when lightning
flashed a forest into ash,
waits at the border
of water and stone—
a pioneer rising where
little else survives.

Such a sky one seldom sees
at other seasons tumbles
an acrobat far above our cares.
If this lake, outcropping, tree, and sky
were all that had been created
it would suffice. But the north
is filled with a sweep
of opulent starkness
stretching from the Great Lakes
to the Mackenzie.

And so an image comes
of a man lost in time,
fishing stream or lake shore
snagged with deadfalls and
sunken logs as if to lure
with an angler's meditative reserve
a better life from below.
Morning comes, its slanting light
closing from sight all that moves
beneath the beaten surface,
all that exists in a breath as
possibilities of air.

After The Months Of Death

After the months of death, spring flocks return,
fill the brittle vines with feathered dark
where sap will soon burst its sugar into
twisted fingers that clutch the iron rail
like drowning sailors who can't relinquish hope.

And so nature resurrects herself;
birds burning with lust court in shadows
where mere weeks ago snow built white mansions.
For as the last shrivelled haw tumbles
into the opening earth, all seeds run

to a new creation. Life soon forgets
the desolation preceding birth—
in that instant, the past lapses beyond knowing.
And the sap returning forgets those days no sap ran.
Spring awakens, and the world breathes green.

Edge

Dune grasses, milkweed,
poplar seedlings,
and wild grape
        torn by wind

have colonized
this ragged edge of sand.

World of hot sun
and drought in summer

ice storms and
gales
        all winter

yet a few plants
survive
each year.

How like love,
these roots
that
        bind
shifting land

to hold it
        whole.

The Willow At The Edge Of The World

Fifteen feet high,
perhaps twenty,
the willow retains
purchase on this bit
of crumbling sand.

Her lowest branches
sweep the ground,
conceal an infant
black locust
striving for sunlight.

Beyond this narrow
strip of stony beach
a few sailboats
race for a horizon
of empty space.

All night the breath
of the nearest star,
improbable lightyears
distant, troubles my willow
in her tenuous sleep.

In Praise Of The Autumn Rose

Dark sounds linger
in the autumn rose
before dawn opens
its petals.

The heart knows best
—always the heart—
in shimmering waters
every end a beginning.

So our winter becomes
a fresh year
under each greening leaf
a thorn of beauty.

Yellow-throated Vireo

Not long before my sixtieth birthday
I was walking along Cumberland Avenue.
Aristotle was on my mind; how
People's Poetry silently suggests a metaphysics,
how goodness implies an order in the soul.
The Equinox was at hand with summer
hanging on, goldenrod still fresh,
still alive. It might have been an afternoon like this
when Robert Sward wrote in "After the Bypass"
of falling into a place where everything
was music.
Noted for his husky song
the yellow-throated vireo, my first-ever sighting,
rises from a yard of wildflowers,
pauses on a telephone wire, then darts off,
a transcendent green on the eve of autumn.

October Morning

Late last night a red hand stole the green from the sumacs along the trail where it begins to climb the mountain.

When you look toward the mills and the water, a hint of mist clings around the harbour's edge, around its quiet darkness, like smoke.

At dawn the Concord grapes so cool, the flavour of night still in their juice, the scent of dark hours: vines holding back the day.

A woman in a white gown stands on her back porch; she watches early cars drive by, hears footsteps in the alley. All the morning's light is for her—

And the daylight moon.

Evening Train

Seven o'clock. Three Susquehanna freighters
and eighty-six cars start
for the Niagara Frontier and beyond.
There is a smell of cracked oil
and the squeal of wheels
as they cross an ungreased switch.
When the last car vanishes down the tunnel
of the westering sun, silence returns
to the autumn flowers, to the ripened corn.

The path of understanding
lies through not knowing.
Pick any blossom along the railbed—
goldenrod, asters, or fading
purple thistle—behind this beauty
lies darkness, lies the mystery
at the heart of all truth. Even the
sentinel trees cannot tell you
how long the train's been gone.

The evening's love song
echoes the canticles of night.
Stepping out of your life
you enter the dark. Your hand closes
the door behind, and you find
your entire journey has brought you here—
to the banks of this river without water,
to this bell ringing
through deep wells of sky.

Pocono Highlands

October's hills
retain a great silence.
Scarlet maples lift boughs
to apple cider light;
not even windshadows stir
between their straight trunks.

Let's inhabit ourselves
in these dense thickets.
Let's follow no path,
but walk where darkness emerges
and fallen leaves
exhale among stones.

For here, where the beauty
of life merges with
the beauty found in decay, can a
fading year open
long-tired eyes to the dazzle
of a blackbird's wing.

Like stoic theologians
pines contemplate
winter's stark advent, await
that knife-edge gust,
while near a creek, wild cherries
blaze with saffron desire.

Walking In An All-day Fog At The Close Of Autumn

Learn of the green world what can be thy place
In scaled invention or true artistry
—Ezra Pound, Canto LXXXI

The mountain has vanished
as have all the trees
on even its lowest slopes.
In the park a few maples
and stolid oaks brandish
their colour in the face
of encircling walls of cloud.

If I stood by the harbour
there would be only the
unbroken grey of mist and water
with no horizon anywhere.
And from beyond the fog
mariners singing in a language
known only to them.

A century and a half ago
nothing but cattails and rushes
where my feet meet
solid earth. Freshwater marsh;
the wind of November
elevating to music these
brittle plants, this brittle air.

The place to the left of my road
could be an orchard of women
collecting windfalls for cider,
their baskets overflowing
with that willing light
the moon will draw to her
as the fog lifts.

The Last Autumn Of The Trees

In memory of the Red Hill Creek Valley

In the last autumn of the trees
salmon, some over three feet long,
fought their way up Red Hill Creek,
through shallows that left their backs exposed,
to spawn. While weary fish struggled to reach
the gravel beds of their birth,
voters decided to uproot their park
and build a truck by-pass to speed
continental trade, the better to
service the American economy.

In the last autumn of the trees
chainsaws startle migrating herons,
awaken white-tailed deer in their
hidden thickets. Century-old hardwoods
fall, even older hemlocks, three feet thick,
crash down slopes where rocks split soil
it required five hundred years to make,
each autumn's scattering of leaves
adding another frail layer,
preparing for another season of hope.

In this season of chainsaws
and bulldozers, coyotes flee
before earth churned to mud,
flee into an urban silence
where the glistening meadow lies stripped
to its bedrock. The dead leave holes where life
had cried out in joy, or pain, or fear.
So a park, a salmon run, enters
the desolation of machines where no leaves
rustle, no snow settles among cattails.

In the marsh about to be drained
cattails comb winter's white hair.
The few remaining maple leaves
paste yellow questions on the wind.
Some say that at mid-winter
an old woman becomes young again,
a willow reliving the green days
of her youth. Raspberry canes
carry purple into the closing season,
to that stillpoint where vision begins.

In the last autumn of the trees
I watched the beautiful fish
return to spawn and perish in the
amber pools of their last sunset.

3

Across Dark Waters

Autumn River Has Found My Heart: Variations on eight poems by Li Po

New willows
spring up
        in abandoned gardens

Chestnuts sing
        spring's unbearable
        song

Only this West River
moon
        inhabits
        Wu Palace.

Exiled by war
I wander
            home
            nowhere

Old rivertown
a flute's pure song
      plum blossoms
      falling   falling.

The river merchant wanders
his boat blown
        by Heaven's winds

blown like a bird
in high clouds
                    sailing away

leaving on earth
no trace.

I walk out naked
among green trees
        my white-feathered fan
        a cloud of morning

Hair tossed
                by pine winds

my hat hangs
on this cliff of air.

Autumn River severs
a thousand mountains

White egrets fill
hidden shallows

Alone
  between Heaven
  and earth

gibbon cries
pierce
  my heart.

September's winds
sweep frontier passes

A Mongol's falcon
  becomes
  a tossed snowflake

so high
so high
  autumn mountains
  fill its eyes.

Moonlight visits my bed
like frost
whitening autumn fields

I dream
my old home
as mountains pass.

Birds all gone—
deep sky forever
I drift
aimless as
day's last clouds

Ching-t'ing Mountain
and I
watch each other

until it alone
remains.

Homage

after Tu Fu

I

A fine day in late autumn, the clear sky
Journeys all the way to the Yangtze's mouth.
This evening a message from Ch'ang-an:
Tibetan armies approach the capital's gates!

With the setting sun I go down
To the river; darkness floods the reeds.
Even the chrysanthemums fail to lift
My spirits with their buoyant colours.

II

I buy some wine and sit amid the rushes.
As night rises from the face of the water,
Screams of disturbed gibbons fill Wu Gorge.
The stars reveal nothing of the future.

My family scattered, my health ruined,
I now know I can never return to the Court.
By midnight the cold wind rending the
Brittle reeds has torn my heart in two.

Two Seasons

poems in honour of
Federico García Lorca

Equinox

All night a cold rain
lashed these hills.
This morning the brook
runs stained by
fallen leaves.

The Equinox comes
and young girls
enter Catholic schools
their eyes bright
autumn gold.

The deepest yellow
of willows
and the still yellow
of the heart
become one.

Blue River

Cast among storm clouds
the falcon
soars like a brief song
to her rocks
and deep mists.

Guarded by steep hills
a still pool
wraps the winter sky
in a quilt
of black leaves.

I wish to be the
blue river
holding winter skies
on my way
to your sea.

Reply To Czeslaw Milosz

So red—that single branch
    of the sugar maple
standing against its still-green
    brothers and sisters—
so red it ignites this grey day
    as if the sun
stood suddenly revealed
    in our forest's dark centre.

Asters burn their purple joy
    despite the frost
and even a few goldenrod plumes
    open yellow florets
as these hills sweep down
    to November.
Wild grapes swell sweet
    with their hoard of sunlight.

Not giving up on philosophy
    I love the visible world
no more than
    the invisible one.
The flash of a blue jay
    for my eyes,
the spirit behind the waterfall
    for my heart;

here, perhaps, is where
　　poetry starts:
in the hunger between reality
　　and its cause.
Today I would speak with the Muse
　　about her old orchard,
how its final apples
　　are red moons filling the night.

The Breath

first Raymond Souster poem

The woodpecker in Ray Souster's backyard
climbs the dying trunk, drums
almost silently while we talk of Louis Dudek
and Charles Olson. It's a Downy Woodpecker,
a female, and a bit undersized. She will remain
the entire winter, feeding on suet hung
beneath the bird feeder. Were Ray not mostly blind
he might write another backyard poem,
place her in it like Olson's kingfishers, but Ray can
neither see nor hear her as she digs for wood borers.

When I met Dudek he was old, tired of fighting
with Layton, struggling with his final works.
"I have left so much undone," he said.
It is there, in those twilight struggles,
one either fails or pleases the Muse,
for the last fruit often yields redemption.
Beneath the bark of the doomed tree
insects think only of survival, only of
eluding the probing beak, while Ray considers
the length of a line, the measure of a poet's breath.

The Manx Shearwater On Lake Ontario

second Raymond Souster poem

On a day remarkable for its lack of birds
we sit in Ray Souster's yard discussing Lowell,
how he made up stories to reveal a truth
pure facts could but obscure. We sip Irish beer
to ease our summer thirsts. A dead silence
fills Ray's trees when conversation halts.
Does it matter Harriet Winslow's home
did not command a view of Penobscot Bay
or that John Winslow was not the Indian Killer?
Surely Josiah Winslow has a grave somewhere.

How to crack the shell of commonplace perception
to reach trees taller than trees, birds freer than birds!
Beyond our inconclusive observations
the planet rotates and its seas continue
their argument with shoreline rocks, their reshaping
of our lives, even this far inland. As we speak
a Manx shearwater is sighted at Van Wagner's Beach,
thirteen hundred miles from its island home
in the North Atlantic off the coast of Newfoundland.
It skims the limit of vision and is gone.

Last Poems

for Pablo Neruda

Winter, like death, arrives
to strip the garden, inter yellowed leaves
beneath the pale flesh of an early snow.
In its solitude, winter brings a kind of freedom
when the book of desire has been read
and the new book of completion
lies as yet unwritten.

In his last poems, Neruda
was a birch tree awaiting the black rain.
Today is the shortest day of the year;
already darkness falls, night's chill
lingering at the windows, a thief
noiseless in the long hours before dawn.
All man's seasons lead to this solstice.

Insects hunt among piled leaves
for the gold of ruined cities.
History lives in the skin of the birches,
each peeling layer revealing winter's truth—
a failing light speaking the language
of withered roses. Before this message
all nature kneels speechless.

Still, a new season germinates
in the moon's shadow.
Rose bushes will again flower
in the kitchen dooryard.
Even those ravaged leaves, chastised
by bitter storms, will rise as a green choir
and return to branch and stem.

With every sip of wine, night's taste lingers.
What vestments become a man
wandering through his garden?
What food justifies his longing
in a world of recovering life?
A sorrow of crows passes overhead,
black wings ring out across still vineyards.

With his language of salt
he restored the heart of the sea.
Winter's signature, like a guitarist's
final note, fades into solitude.
Land of deep mountains: all that remains
is the rose, its thorns releasing the pain
of earth's slow return from exile.

Taproots

a farewell for
Pablo Neruda

When love departs
fire deserts our earth
and the heart turns to stone.
I am still here
yet our world revolves
as if all were mere chance.
Today my elm,
tomorrow my ash,
praise the returning sun.

And you, Pablo,
embrace this evening
the land of your fathers.
In your heart's core
are little stories
of pain and resilience.
Today your oak,
tomorrow your larch,
praise the returning rain.

Should a people ever
give up their language
they surrender their soil.
The night's rain frees
from silence the speech
of a thousand good-byes.
Let your poems
be the taproot that
pierces Chile's stone husk.

The Pacific rages
throughout the winter
with no help from the gods.
The Andes stand
without being asked
against the sky's terrors.
You are all seas
you are all mountains
you are a ship of bells

ringing across dark waters.

The Sorrow Of God

a morning poem for
Robert Bly

I awake at dawn to a day of frozen sleet,
a cold day at the end of February
with the mountain's face buried in cloud.

It's so early no one else seems to be up;
then I hear a car start, its engine warming
by the house next door. Silently the mists lift.

I read last night that a moment of sorrow
preceded creation, that act that summoned
the Earth into being, and us with it.

The house finches have already returned;
I see them waiting on the telephone wire.
My neighbour enters his car and drives off.

My mountain ash stands locked in a ring of ice,
but the night's wind has dropped to nothing.
Later, I suspect, this ice will melt.

The day's still quiet, my children asleep
in their rooms under the eaves. And I cannot
in my moment of time believe in a god of sorrow.

James Wright Looks At A Lake Long After The Oaks Have Turned

The borderland in November,
darkness below the grey surface,
darkness behind the scudding clouds.

Thoughtlessly smoking the Pall Malls
that will kill him,
Jim takes out his pen

and there are whales,
dolphins leaping into discovery,
waiting with the poet for night.

But vision cannot redeem him;
always fear and anger
arise, always his self-loathing

lies beneath the waters of the lake,
beneath the sheet of paper
where the poem is yet unwritten.

A spring-fed Minnesota lake,
opaque, waiting to receive
the season's first snow.

Jim stands where rushes whistle
and icy waters clutch the shore,
driven in by a coming storm.

The darkness within will not break.
It forms a ladder he'll climb
year by year to death's embrasure.

A farmhouse stands among its fall trees,
the windows letting out the light
while welcoming in our night.

Reading Dickinson While Listening To Schubert's 3rd

As imperceptibly as grief
The summer lapsed away
—Emily Dickinson

I

Birds fill the boxelder
with song as the coming
evening sweeps away
the afternoon's heat.

Soon streetlights will be lit;
the final workmen will
reach home trailing
the blue night behind them.

II

Every season must end
so another will be born.
Before long, autumn roses
replace summer's varieties.

Even now asters make ready,
goldenrod summons the sun
a little later each morning,
the smoke of October waits.

III

At fifty-five she was buried
near the Homestead
at the time rhododendron
and orchis bloom.

All her love lay
bound up on two thousand
scraps of notepaper
concealed from view.

IV

The scent of basswood
softens the night,
its flowers, favoured
by bees above all others,

catch the least breeze within
a hive of cream-coloured petals,
the way a wayward heart
can be caught by the first stars.

V

Schubert's *3rd Symphony*
foreshadows his *9th*,
beckons possibilities vague
as a summer's stars

veiled by a haze of heat.
In his music he opens
his heart to all the grief
of this world, and all its joy.

In Celebration Of Kenneth Rexroth: Two Brief Autumn Poems

Japanese Maples

Although the tuliptree's leaves are down,
 maples so redden the wind

 even the frost draws back
and the nightshade's lanterns go out one by one.

The Darkness Between

After a week of overcast skies
 first stars appear,

 the darkness between
a bird calling from the lake at night.

Dreaming Of Jack Gilbert

I dreamt of you last night, Jack.
You were reading in an art gallery,
polished wood floors, wide-planked
and glowing. The paintings were of the '50s.
New York. Jazz-inspired.

A storm that had been building all day
broke later that evening, then
subsided slightly. You would not know
Pittsburgh should you return. So much
has changed, so much has vanished.

Perhaps we cannot hold memories
together or defend what is good
in the life of a city. You moved
to Greenwich Village to write of Orpheus.
The seasons turn without regard for us.

In my dream you were tired, Jack,
an old man even older than I am now,
white-bearded and heavy;
yet you were married to a
much younger woman.

She and I stood in the fields of rain
talking about Paros, Kos, and the poems
you wrote there years ago.
Inside the gallery you read to the night,
great fires still burning in your voice.

American Poetry

I

In the still hours I'm reading
"The Kingfishers"   again,

how one might find honey
among stones.

The forces of earth named us,
granted speech to dry tongues;

even the summer night
awaits us.

No, not us, but our words
rolling like stones,

like thunder before rain,
for it is by words we are known.

Hoofbeats ring the temple's
black arch;

a journey without witnesses
begins.

We ride all night
to face the morning sun

when it rises from the sea's embrace,
the brutality of its tongues

of flame.

II

But the birds, great flocks of birds
rose straight into the setting sun

just like the Europeans
who came later

sailed for the burning tongues
across the North Atlantic

and were cast astray by the madness
of the sea.

And us? We refuse to grieve when
our train stops

and we must set out on foot
across dark prairies.

The continent contains countless
lost rivers,

their waters flow through the night,
murmur around stones.

Our hands begin to glow
with starlight;

our blood is absorbed
into the landscape, into miles of grass

rising.

On First Looking Into Allen's The New American Poetry

for Don Allen

I

That you chose to open
with Olson's "The Kingfishers"
showed

a willingness to lead
your readers

into America, the real
America.

Which was not
the America of Frost
or Sandburg

but an America without
dreams

devoid of that
honeyed vision.

Always before
that doubled vision—
what is, what should be

now only the "is"
survives

a tough stick of shagbark
hickory.

Not hope abandoned
but no hope to crutch us
onward

to a land with
more death than love

with a past that cannot be forgotten,
a future always unknowable.

So night comes
like Europe from the east
and a purple sky

quiets the singing trees
down by the harbour

if you would find America here
then hunt.

II

That you chose to close
with Meltzer's "Prayerwheel"
displayed

a faith in the mortality
of America

the mortality of New York,
city of visions.

What then is the fate
of man and woman
or of man and woman together

    but a way to measure
    the transit of history

    the decay
    of time?

If you would
seek the garden on Broadway
my fond regards

    and safe passage
    on your neon way

    but, you will never find
    Whitman there.

Nor the poetry that redeems
the dream of the new Jerusalem
of a poet's desire

    for desire here
    is merely sexual

    is the roar of the subway
    in its tunnel of night.

It is not love
that will save America
nor the lack of love

    we are eager
    to go into blindness

    why not (he asks)
    die alone?

4

The Flute Coming Down From the Mountains

The Carpenter's Son

It's spring in the mountains,
almost honeysuckle time,
when the carpenter dies
and is placed under a weeping elm
next to his father.
His widow refusing to touch them,
the tools that blessed his hands
are packed away and
laid to rest in the attic by a neighbour.

All night with its tongue of longing
the wind presses along
a roof of shingles his hands first cut,
and the planks of his bedroom floor
darken like his heart's silent chambers.
Looking down on the town,
nailheads he hammered shine
in constellations of sorrow.
Yet his work remains unfinished.

He was the valley's only carpenter
and no one will take his place.
Solitude fills the summer and
autumn's leaves colour and fall
without the sound of saws.
Snow exiles both town and forest,
buries the widow in her bed of dreams.
She grieves alone, her only child
long vanished into another country.

At dawn, the carpenter's son
awakens in a field
where no house has ever stood.

Silence In The Fields Of Autumn

The harp of rain falls quiet.
Drifted maple leaves form a city of light
spread within the shadows
of a copper beech.
Last summer's insects,
like all true nomads,
have gone; only silence remains.

I enter the city of light
where grass leans into winter.
When I look at my hand
I see fields that go on forever,
a distant sea too far away to know.

If I stand here all afternoon
dusk will enter my body,
mix with my blood
to awaken the heart's sorrow.
By then no one will be able to resist
the flute coming down from the mountains.

It is an old friend I had almost forgotten
returning after many years
in this season of need.

In Jean Joubert's Kitchen

Le poème ici né du matin …

Steep your morning tea
my friend;

don't mind that cat
lurking outside your door.

Why lament the fleeing seasons
when we can embrace

the winter of silence?
An old woman walks

the cobbled streets carrying
November's rain in her heart.

Her voice is that of the ocean
falling into the salt of its tears.

Out of the cold dawn
poems appear,

dark planets where yesterday
the orchard stood bare.

Connecticut Winter

Too early for bed,
too exhausted for work,
I watch evening cover
western Connecticut.
Moon and stars lie
concealed by clouds;
only darkness remains
welling up from silence.

I walk among woodlots.
Narrow bridges span
creeks imprisoned in ice.
Bells of frozen iron
hang in country steeples.
From barren fields
rises that formless grief
our night calls brother.

Adoration & Prayer

Adoration

I would bring a gift to the silent village
perhaps rain at midnight
or stripped trees awaiting
the year's first snow.

Prayer

Let my tongue be the stonemason's hammer
let red haws light the field
when no leaves are left
to show us we were here.

Rain

The rain brings her darkness
    to the river.
If you listen for the harp
    a voice is crying
while in every window
    a memory of the moon.

Only a dry country
    can value rain,
the rush of it
    hissing across a roof,
wet fingers
    on the high windows.

The harpist stands
    by some empty barges,
the pull of water
    releasing the night
like a vagrant raft
    heading to New Orleans.

Harbour

Now that summer
is almost at hand
the reedbeds
fill with dreams.
They shine like stars
falling to earth
or like sparks
from old paddlewheelers.

This is how cities
were erected—
a boat stopped
and men built a dock.
Even dreams become real
when turned to lumber,
every stone step
an act of praise.

Where great furnaces
blaze through our night
trees will rise up,
their black leaves
conversing with
the worn moon.
Deep in the harbour
we live among bells.

Black Maps

How long will a stick
    tossed from this span
take to reach the Gulf?
    Or does it get trapped
in an oxbow
    above Natchez,
the river's eddies
    counterclockwise turning
the way
    King Biscuit Boy
could turn a blues lick
    on a dime?

No one can say
    where these maps
will carry us—
    black roads
across black counties,
    the tupelo holding back
a sky full of rain.
    Old Possum said
the river is a God;
    where long grasses
wade in the water
    a woman is singing.

Rain In July

Rain echoes
through the blind galleries
of night.

Everywhere is a long way off,
seemingly abandoned
to the infinite distance.

Quincy Jones plays
"Cast Your Fate to the Wind"

I hear his trumpet
behind rolls of thunder.

The woman standing at the
corner of Barton
has vanished

even her cigarette

even her black
glove.

Sunken Boats

I

The rowboat swamped at lake's end
holds all the water of the sky.
When the storm arose
the tuliptree's flowers clenched like fists.
Now their reflections
hang along the shoreline,
a row of drowned gods.
Only the black oarsman dares remember
the creak of wood on wood,
the voices of sailors calling down the stars.

II

The moon reflected in the dark canal
is a boat sailing where we cannot follow.
The lily pads scarcely move.
And the footsteps of the
bride and groom fade into midnight.
One can only think of
Miró's love of Machado,
their moon a honeycomb worked by bees,
an emblem they've nailed
to the mast of the night.

III

What is old blood
but the closure of the heart?
Wood rots among leaves and reeds,
paint blisters. The fishermen
have forsaken their pale rituals,
their hands have flown off
beyond the horizon. Seasons pass
until keels and ribs lie exposed
to gather all the stars
of a summer's night,
all the snow
of a December storm.

Only the bride moves now
reaching across still waters
to open the bones of the sea.

Here

Because space itself, not only matter,
was all contained within the pinpoint
that preceded the Big Bang,
the correct answer to the question
'Where did it take place?' is
'here'.

—Prof. Timothy Ferris

So it starts at this place
where I write these lines—
the Creator's hand moved
and all was summoned into being
in six days, or fifteen billion years,
or even one single, breathless instant.
I lie beside my sleeping wife,
rain dripping through the roof
having forced me from my study,
and sense the beauty of a will
greater than all that is known.

Outside, trees dance in their
wet skins; the first storm of spring
sweeps up from the southwest.
A season of death ends, blackened drifts
sink into their soil, stars return
from their dark zodiac, from the
mouth through which winter howled.
Where the remains of the marsh
still lie behind the candy factory
a grief of willows weeps into the earth.

Things must finish where they start;
each ending a beginning, each life lived
returning, changed, made noble
by morning's sun. And in the dazzle
every kernel of rain among the willow's hair
reveals its own sun, its opening and closing.
Where land and water merge
I stand watching migrating geese
worship the air with their wings.

Only love can bind our lives together.
As water becomes mud, soil runs
among a generation of cattails rising up.
Where the footpath verges on the far shore
a tree of birds calls into daylight
the world their song has made their own.

Reaching The Ocean

Travelling south all morning
I finally reach the ocean
and suddenly the land looks small.
Beyond a stone jetty—only sky,
water, and the tang of brine;
only this endless azure
effortlessly filling the world.

It's like the second day of Creation—
God separating the blue of the sea
from the purer blue of Heaven;
or perhaps the generous, blue heart
of God making paradise actual.
Such a day arrives as a gift
like a south wind in January,
or forgiveness.

Bone Flute

The voice of a half moon
        sitting in the locust tree
is the sound of white silk
        drawn through a wedding ring.
Cootes Paradise cloaked by vapours,
        its sorrow seeping into reeds—
everywhere moon and mist,
        the man and his flute going home.

5

Nobody But You

Love Where Our Nights Are Long

for Gilda

I

Look into my heart
and take what you want,
all I need is to be next to you
as dawn enters the window.

II

After a night of love
we awaken to make love again;
the scent of you still lingering
as I steep our morning tea.

III

Late January; at last winter arrives—
snow lies on the sumac branches
while you lie in my arms,
my cock stiffening again.

IV

With hands on your belly I enter you
slowly at first, then faster,
unable to hold back until our hairs
fuse in a cascade of flame.

V

The River of Heaven cuts the sky in two—
your cries of passion sever our night
as they rise sharper and sharper
from these damp sheets.

VI

Snow drifts through a garden
where last month flowers were everywhere.
The chrysanthemums are brittle now;
only your body warms these cold days.

VII

A sliver of moon low in the west,
the night bitter, without wind.
Our lives pass, season to season,
two lovers become one.

VIII

I wait for you, my desire ever more desperate.
Unlike the yellow coltsfoot,
often faded within a week, our lust
burns brighter after twenty years.

IX

The taste of your come
still fresh in my mouth,
we lie exhausted in day's first light,
notice the songbirds have returned.

X

After climbing Hamilton Mountain
you look so beautiful, so *breathless*,
I want to take you right here
where snowbanks overlook our city.

XI

Reading John Clare's poem of the fallen elm
I suddenly need you. Come,
we must spend the afternoon entangled
until exhaustion stills my quaking heart.

XII

All at once you come
and wonder brims my mouth;
if only I could look into your eyes
at this instant!

After Work

for Gilda

Both house and woods
lie under a nearly naked moon.
Midnight arrives
and the work of the day
is finally complete.

I drink wine
while you sleep beside me;
watch the frost as it comes
down from the mountain.
The trees are black with ice.

My beard has grown white;
our daughters will soon
be young women.
At our window
the winter wind calls.

Sulphuric

The Soo Line diesel pulling the acid train
bakes in July's heat.
Its smell of spattered oil reaches
the workers' homes.
All the day's darkness has been driven
into the trees.

Where Venetian blinds shut out the sun, a woman
and her young man
toss in their sweat, in the sorrow
of their own salt.
Only the daylight moon, emerging from her lake,
can sing this day.

Walking To The Eramosa During The Time Of Harvest

for Katherine L. Gordon

Our path parallels the river
through white cedar groves and
mixed Carolinian hardwoods,
runs near an old Indian camp
where the Neutrals once passed by.
A glacial valley gouged through limestone
when ice mountains walked the land;
a forest of cedar duff and
maidenhair ferns, the watercress
still green a week past equinox.

After a wet September, the land
lies rain-logged, each human step sinking
into experience more sacred
than mere language can extol.
Soon will come the first sharp days;
the Festival of the Autumn Moon
will bring harvest's gathering in.

We slowly walk this path to water
where lovers quicken and collapse
in sibilant riverrun afternoons.
Overhead a scud of cloud and drizzle
rides a wind we cannot feel,
a gust like a held kiss, bound tight
in imagination's green sanctuary,
in that echoing silence our moon
will soon rise through.

Late October At Rockwood

for Katherine L. Gordon

I

Forests flame above these river-cut cliffs
when sunlight strikes through cloudrifts throwing
colours into the Eramosa River.
Far below, Nashville warblers and the
always-hidden winter wrens breed where limestone
filters water pure. American beech
cast yellow leaves into a rising wind.

Deep in the valley, the scent of woodfires
lingers. Black ash shadow moist bottomlands:
wood for barrel staves and farmers' baskets, the
dark heartwood singing through our moonless nights.
Even at this peak of autumn, winter
rises—each cold spring hungering for snow.

II

This is the last holdout against winter;
leaves of fire spot the river like tiny
suns that would light our flight from the stone grasp
of winds off the Prairies, but like these birch
we shall stare the season down. Old age strikes
all in an instant, like autumn's first frost.

Our years turn from death to re-birth, but at
their final dying all things transform to
other things: trees become beaver, our earth
will make new stars. Leaves of sugar maples
whirl into space: echoes of creation's
beauty. Let the blood of this earth run quick
'til ice clots its creeks and our surging hearts.

Quilts

All day snow came and went
like the bitter wind down from James Bay
until by dusk it stuck to grass
and my neighbour's roof, a revenant
of winters past. Just the willow now
retains its leaves so deeply
into November—that and
a scatter of oaks turned rawhide
by the cold. In January of '71
snow drifted over 12 feet deep
in the Ottawa Valley's towns;
people used bedroom windows
to go and come. And a blue tint
coloured the snowbanks in late
afternoon like some hidden desire,
like quilts passed down mother
to daughter, quilts waiting silently
in the chill of those dark hours,
wind rising through naked branches.

Listening To The Women Of The Wind

The wise woman lives in the grass,
is in the seeds of the grass
on this headland overlooking
the far western tip of Lake Ontario.

The spirit of the wild woman
resides in the geese heading south
and in the cormorants drying their wings,
going nowhere.

At the back of the north wind I hear
the rustle of the goddess' skirts,
the lilt of her laughter
floating free over the escarpment.

A female black-throated blue warbler
perches on a staghorn sumac;
any day the leaves will commence
to redden. When the white maiden

sweeps down from Hudson Bay,
we'll see her harsh, sharp beauty
in the inlets where the lake freezes,
we'll learn her icy wisdom.

But today is the Autumnal Equinox;
walnuts drop their green spheres
into a field of goldenrod, a few
lingering monarchs pass through the trees.

Even the noisy geese fall silent.
I sit still, so still
a vulture scans me twice
before moving on.

North Of The Great Lakes

Who can love this land
shackled by stone and winter?

A Scot from Wester Ross?
The Icelander? Fishermen
blown in from the Faeroes?

Who can love the silence
of black lakes imprisoned by pines?

Too far north for gardens,
too little summer for corn,
each warm day hoarded shamelessly.

And it seems never enough
to comfort the human heart.

Kettle bog, quartz outcrop,
marks glaciers gouged
across exposed stone.

So hard to make a living
one can't tell whether to leave

or stay. A jawbone land,
its stern beauty enticing
us into pain.

Who can love this land?
The Swede? The Russian D.P.?

Gravel roads connecting
bush towns, mining camps
a hundred miles apart—

one could die here and
never be found save by accident.

One comes upon ponds
without names
emerging from a cedar's shade

like some movement
suddenly by darkness visible

and the day's luminous
as if a sunfire sea
swept the land.

Then silence closes like a fist
so cold the stones ache.

Autumn grieves in early dark—
leaves rattle over rock,
like hapless missionaries.

In the Jesuit night
the funeral season begins.

Frozen streams embrace
the land's bare ribs,
blue shadows bruise the snow.

So far north of summer,
only love can save this land.

Going Off The Road Near Bishops Mills

Because the car
went off the road
I learned the softness
of snow

and its compressibility,
how it could halt
a ton of steel
and glass

without a sound
or single scratch.
Because the car
took off

to enter a new world,
a world where
animals could live
without fear,

a place free
of human noise,
I understand
that I, too,

must enter
another world,
a world where
nothing lives

but necessity.

And because
    the silence came
so the night hung
    like a blazing star

above the stubblefields,
    I could see that
the hand guiding all
    guides me;

for in this land
    of winter farms
coldly drifted
    above the St. Lawrence

the year's cruelty
    is buried and
the dark daughters
    banished to their

long white homes.
    Because the car
went off the road
    the land in beauty

lay, and my heart
    rang like a bell
through the iron air,
    so the great wheel

turning its seasons
    towards spring
came 'round,
    the earth breathing

beneath my feet
	like a proud woman
awakened to passion
	by the dawn sun's

flaming hands.

6

A Rain of Grief

Heading For The Depot

Nine hours of driving
through downtown streets; snowbanks,
pedestrians everywhere, school children,
red lights, stop signs. Shaken to the teeth
by a pair of used-up shocks.

Old worn GMC delivery truck—
worn as my hard-luck back, the bad
tendon in my right knee—
one hundred and seventeen stops,
and a heater that will not work.

Finally, the last customer;
darkness, that post-rush-hour quiet.
Heading back to the depot
my road relaxed of traffic, the fiery tongues
of steelmills above the harbour's ice.

Abattoir

Still dark outside, yet the stench of death
is everywhere, sickly sweet
and penetrating. The fear in their eyes
burns so fiercely it will dog you
all the days of your life, so don't look.
An older Jewish woman I know
lived through the Nazi death camps
to write poems in Toronto,
but in this Auschwitz for animals
there are no survivors.

We pull organs from partly eviscerated bodies—
kidneys, livers, the lungs rich with uncirculated blood,
and finally the stilled heart.
Here death is graceless.
This is how dawn comes to east Hamilton;
this is what the animals pay
that we may eat.

Autumn Winds

At Cootes Paradise
autumn winds burn maples
scarlet during the night.
The young mother pushing a pram
or students cutting chemistry class
discover burnished colours
where yesterday only geese
sang to the chilling sky.

On Burlington Street
stunted thistles shake.
Red is the dead colour of steelsheds
that rattle when frost rides winds
cut only by guywires and
the broken-windowed night.
Red is the hunger of families
without work.

A man asks *what is beauty?*
The day tells one truth,
night another, final truth.
Winter clouds gather beyond the mills.
When the hand is pulled from the cross
red is a wind pouring from the hole
a nail made. It is a shout
of rusty metal filling our sky.

Smith's Knoll

The life of the dead is placed
in the memory of the living.
—Cicero

It's from Manchester they came,
from Birmingham, from Sheffield—
ploughboys released from their land
by the enclosures or
the unneeded children of the industrial poor
with nothing to do but starve.
With no plough to follow, no sheep to herd,
they followed their empty stomachs
across a land that no longer wanted them
into an urban dark that could not use them.
Eventually those who had not died
signed on to march for their Hanoverian King
in exchange for his promise
of a pound of meat and a loaf of bread per day.

So one day they marched into this
maple and elm wilderness on the edge
of a lake great as a sea,
and knew not where they were or why,
marching in wool on a hot June day
in a bath of sweat and mosquitoes.

Or they came from Kentucky or Virginia;
freckle-faced farmlads after adventure
or searching out a better future
in the territory north of the Great Lakes.
They found this field and pitched camp
by a creek with a wild rose border
almost ready to bloom, and the sweet scent
of flowering black locust spread over all.
For they were young men in the summer
of their lives, happy, perhaps,
as young men usually are to be alive
and on the move.

And yet they were surprised out of their lives
in the night of their sleep by the silent bayonet
or a hatchet releasing the brain's heartwood
from its dome of bone. Then the darkness was ablaze
with a confusion of musket fire so that
ploughboy clutched ploughboy
as they fell together into this anonymous spot
leaving their names behind, leaving
their pumping blood to sanctify this land—
the sons of Wiltshire and the sons
of the Blue Grass State
joined in Death's brotherhood.

All that was known to mothers
and sweethearts in England and America
was this: some returned from Upper Canada,
some did not.
And in the funeral earth
they lay these fleeting generations
without names or nations, unprayed for,
a jumble of marrowless bones
where wild roses are about to bloom
and robins call and the mosquitoes
winnow the summer air.

So we gather here this Sunday morning
one hundred and eighty-seven years
after American cannon fired from this knoll
to deliver, so prematurely, the souls
of young men to their maker.
Perhaps their soldiers' spirits see us now
as we stand ambiguous at their fresh grave:
Lieutenant Colonel Bob Barnes of the King's Regiment,
Major Simon Bailey, Royal Gloucestershire,
Berkshire, and Wiltshire Regiment,
Colonel Karen McClellan, United States Army,
Lieutenant Colonel Rick Mount Pleasant,
Canadian Forces—and this poet, citizen
of the United States, yet loyal subject
of Queen Elizabeth II — and just perhaps
the dead can hear *Last Post* and *Taps* played
while the single wooden box of bones,
draped in the flags of two nations,
containing the only remains of
"about" twenty-one men,
is finally buried in consecrated ground.

As we pray their souls
towards Heaven's peace,
we understand that we are as ambiguous
as these lost boys, who fell as enemies
to lie as brothers in their common coffin.
With our silent thoughts, and even our tears,
these soldiers of forgotten identity,
uncertain nationality, undocumented purpose
lie now and forever
in the wild rose shade.

Cardinal

The day after the *Iroquois*
left Halifax for the Persian Gulf
the cardinal returned to my
black locust. I did not see him
but heard his call before dawn
as I went out to bring in
the news of the coming war.

I did not see him
only his song told of the coming spring,
of his joy at being here,
each season as fresh as a cardinal's flight.

A new war for a new century?
No. The same old war turning
round and round again.
Still, that cardinal's voice
filled the bare branches with light
to bring this February morning
into being.

Stopping By The River At Thanksgiving

Along the Allegheny the trees
stand bare save for a rattle of
rawhide oaks defying wind and frost.
I have come three hundred miles
at Thanksgiving to watch here
where mountains fade to foothills.

An autumn haze lingers, and I too
hesitate as if contemplation
would ease the daily news of war,
as if my heart would not be torn
by the slaughter of young men whose crime
is but to love their land too much.

Thanksgiving. The river cold and blue,
an east wind bearing the scent of snow,
of winter's frozen blood. Hidden jays
cry out again and again
and still the sky is too remote,
these hills too wild for comfort.

On a path by the bank carpeted
in gold and red, my footfalls
flush the hunted deer. Can anger ever
be redeemed? I cannot hear the bombs
yet on the far side of our world
bodies pile like snow in exiled mountains.

Siblings

The Tigris unwinds a ribbon of death.
Basra, Baghdad, Tikrit, Mosul
are footprints of anguish,
are pits of flame where burning feet
stepped. The Jabal Hamrin vanish
under waves of smoke;
only small charred bones remain
where a school, a playground stood.

This is a land the Destroyer swept,
burnt beyond all recognition,
its mosques violated, its history looted.
Only DNA will reveal
the birthplace of civilization;
only the uncallused heart will know
these dismembered corpses
to be our true brothers and sisters.

The pain of their bodies speaks to us
in a tongue we have long forgotten;
their eyes witness a life we cannot imagine.
When, years from now, you meet
on the far side of great waters
the stare of those with flesh scorched black
in your name, by your army,
oh what will you say?

Clay Jars

After a year no one seems to remember
the war

our lives go on while our soldiers die
without comment

there is no daily body count
no claim

of victory or defeat, almost no news
at all.

The war is like that final light
of summer

as it fades to autumn, to the silence
of frost

our dead shrivel with the October leaves
to be

crushed under the feet of school children
skipping home.

It is difficult to know what to do about
the dead

they vanish like clay jars of water spilled
in a desert

the dead whirl in a dust cloud like
wild birds

at night sand fills their throats
forever.

Each flag-draped coffin contains
a brother

our glass dreams bring a rain
of grief

what can grow today to redeem
our losses

when even the stars weep within
bruised clouds?

Praying With The Quakers On The Solstice

Love of enemy is not an optional platitude.
It is how I can discover myself to be
created in the image and likeness of God,
whose love embraces all beings ...
—James Loney

We form a circle just before Christmas;
a single candle illuminates the room
on this longest night of the year. Our thoughts
join the hostages on the far side
of the world, prisoners of a nation
we do not know, a world of deadly faith.
We don't face death every day, as they do;
our faith is not tested, as theirs is.
We cannot imagine their struggle
against darkness or their sustaining love.

A simple, unadorned room; wooden chairs,
straight-backed, functional; a deep stillness
where one might meet God. Here prayers are offered
amid chants and silence. And I wonder
how many turn to religion when all else
fails and only God remains. For we can't
rescue our friend, he has travelled beyond us,
beyond our experience, into the horror
that is Baghdad, called there by a love
stronger than fear. Finally, we join hands
in one last prayer, return to our winter night.

An Offering Of Hope For James Loney

A hundred days have gone since you
in darkness fell
into that stony place human hands
can hardly reach
held in some cell of agony
where hatred flows in poisoned rivers
towards the sea.

Mesopotamia, the Fertile Crescent
of our storybooks—
your faith in the Christ
led you there to spread His mercy
in a land of shattered children
whose decomposing dreams
feed only maggots of despair.
Mesopotamia, where once a single rose
became a garden, today
a single corpse becomes a slaughtered village.

Back home, sharp iris tongues
spear earth's frozen silence;
a purity of snowdrops
signals the season of Lent,
when Jesus entered the wilderness,
His knees bending to unrelenting stone.
A murder of crows,
present in our city all winter,
retreats with its bleak lamentations.

Our sleeping forests awaken;
myrtle warblers and song sparrows arrive
bearing flames borrowed from the sun.
Through green fires of spring,
a fresh Creation draws us
nearer His Passion and
His forgiveness.

Saturday Morning With Sulak

for Sulak Sivaraksa

As though by some cast spell, the pollution's swept away
and late summer dazzles, every blossom glowing
with joy. Such freedom from the cares of struggle!
We are released, or so it seems, like hornets
seeking the sweetest of the windfall pears.
Behind City Hall, Whitehern stands foursquare
in morning silence as if some stained glass artist
caught it in a window full of light, a day without despair.

Yet the new century begins where our old one died:
wars surround the globe, the sweetest lies grace the lips
of Presidents and Ministers of National Defence.
Beyond the porch the canna drives its spearpoint
through tight soil, every excessive lily
bursting vivid against a flawless sky. Over the harbour
herring gulls and black terns dive for fish;
we listen while Mayor Di Ianni speaks of peace.

The secular world reels past the grandeur October brings.
Steel haulers lumber east along Main Street;
trees plump with migrating birds tower over all.
You speak of breathing, of thinking with the body,
not the intellect: "I breathe therefore I am."
And we sit like would-be Buddhas inhaling, exhaling
the long nature of our being. Begonias linger
and lobelia bears its blue banner into autumn.

So still, yet you live engaged, enraged
with fierce, non-violent flames. Action without anger,
the courage to cast aside all fear. We know
the torture victim dies behind barbed-wire
as we talk, the Member of Parliament
helpless at our side. In this garden insect-
hollowed trees still bear fruit, one branch flourishing
with leaves abundant enough to nourish old roots.

Canada's democracy, bourgeois and corrupt,
crumbles daily, while your people grew ancient
before mine began. The Enlightenment stands
emptied out, poisoned by its Cartesian roots,
no branch alive enough to produce edible fruit.
Every flower knows its bee, every bee ecstatic
to be alive and free. And you, my friend, stride free
where summer lingers amid unfamiliar trees.

Crossing The Piedmont Again

A hot Sunday in July,
driving across the Piedmont
passed fields that were tobacco
    in my youth, but
now turned to corn or feed grains.
Cows under trees,
dusty farmyards in after-church silence
almost a month without rain.

Rolling east to the Chesapeake—
salt smell,
    pitch pines in sand.
The Old Dominion.

Sic semper tyrannis.
A summer's sun tossed
    on bright waves.
Intercoastal Waterway,
Havre de Grace to Newport News.

Not far away
the President sits over maps
dreaming of the next war,
    his next invasion.

7

From Roses of Death

A Bridge In Pittsburgh

for Gerald Stern

Day of no school; no homework; no chores.
I'm walking across the 6th Street Bridge in snow
to reach the North Side and Olga Snyder's
Books and Magazines on Federal Street
where I will buy *Side Street* and *Sound of a City*
by James T. Farrell and a science-fiction collection
edited by Judith Merril, whom I will meet
twenty years later in Toronto at a café on Spadina.
Her anthology will cost all of 15 cents, and
the two Farrells will go for 20 cents each.

Later I will read about Heinie Mueller and his wife
living over Calumet in Chicago in their
third-floor walk-up and of three Americans in Paris;
but for now it's the bridge slanting through storm,
and the grey river lifting its barges into frozen air
on a Saturday afternoon in January. At mid-river
the city's towers are lost in gusting flakes,
the grimy brick storefronts along Federal
not yet in sight. And I'm above these cold waters
the Allegheny's brought down from its mountains.

One might expect to meet Whitman
on a day like this, his pockets crammed with poems,
his arms waving as he strides through clouds
reciting his love for Lincoln, his faith in America.
The snow falls thicker now, blotting out
the tugs moored against the far bank, and shrouding
the occasional walker hunched into the wind.
Behind me rise the hills of fire where coal smoulders
deep underground, the snow never sticking
along fissures where hot fumes rise.

These are the hills of my youth,
the hills I will leave behind in smoke and flame.
But today I'm straddling a river I can barely see,
thinking of the dust of used books, of hissing
steam radiators, of the plump old woman
in her shapeless sweater at the scarred desk.
It seems as though my entire world is swaying
high above the Allegheny, above the glowing hills,
pungent with intimacy. It seems as if
this is my only day, the only life to live.

Pale Hand

In memoriam: Hew Charles Torrance,
1859–1931

Winter, and the mill
at the close of the street
draws the curtain of night,
becomes a bird at dusk
vanishing into stillness
where cloud and river meet.
The few houses where people
still have money
send coal smoke
to join the great factory smokes
streaming eastward
in January's wind.

Winter, and the street
is the pale hand of a bride,
its snow pure
as if darkness had never
placed its signature
at the foot of her day.
Behind lighted windows
the unobserved lives
of Slovakian families
continue day by day;
all conversation lost
in a silence of snow.

November's Flames

To portray a city is beyond ending ...
—W. Eugene Smith, 1918–1978

I *Iron Labyrinth*

Staghorn sumacs flame in a fistful of wind
where South Oakland meets its river.

Fires light the end of autumn;
only the Cathedral of Learning rises above their smoke.

Some say this city is a woman—
some day I'll feel her fiery touch, her breath of stars.

We enter the iron gate of November,
on every side the great mills rejoice.

All night the J & L Works pours its crimson
into the river, our one true life.

Let us rake the cast down leaves together
and ignite the future with the day.

II *For the Love of Coke*

Railroad tracks vanish into that place
where the Monongahela swings beyond its trees.

Every year the city yearns to return
to the land's embrace, to its common wealth.

Dancing in the heat of roasting coke
every breath becomes a barb of rusted wire.

You throw your arm up to protect your face
when the ovens flare like the sun.

All afternoon the house fills with
the smell of cabbage and pork drippings.

Drinking Bourbon backed by beer, we know
the end of the day, the end of a life.

III Where a World Begins

Behind the housing projects
the earth falls away to J & L South Side.

What would it be like to tumble into sin
like these sweethaw leaves sailing over the cliff?

After charging the open hearth, swab your blisters,
imagine taking your girl amid asters and goldenrod.

Children play at tightrope walking;
their dreams merge with a river of smoke.

There is only the river drifting through autumn,
and these glowing leaves blowing into another world.

Every day we pry open a door into darkness
to discover one more reason for living.

IV Ponzie's Cafe

On the street a brand new Chevy noses into
the year Joseph McCarthy will die; the year I enter puberty.

When a cold dawn breaks over Homestead
the river's many ghosts enter us.

Hunger hides in the heart of the wife
home alone during the late shift.

Throughout the stark hours the steel runs red
in the slab mill, the continuous blood of a city.

If there were no grief here, could there ever be forgiveness?
How many nights can we lie in bed without touching?

Sumacs and asters will remain;
even in the deep snow, sumacs and asters.

Kaufmann's Dining Room

Pittsburgh during the Eisenhower years
was Don Larsen's perfect game, our new prosperity,
and holiday shopping at Kaufmann's.
Overlooking the city from the eleventh floor
we lunched on fruit cocktail, well-done roast beef,
and berry pie while smoke blew ceaselessly
down river bank and boulevard.

Although the musicians and their palms
had long departed, the Big Store still glowed
Edwardian and stolid, recalling another age
of dilating hopes. Perhaps Republican America
could bring back Rowanlea and Edgehill.
Looking through the windows of the great hall
while sopping gravy with pure, white bread
(not Town Talk, but something better, more *deluxe*)
all things seemed forthcoming.

Back then Pittsburgh always balanced on the verge
of something more deluxe. Scarred by ten lost years
and combat producing survivors only when victory
called forth crowds to cheer, both city and nation
were trapped in their terminal becoming.
If Gould's Wabash fantasy still stood
a condemned Beaux-Arts ghost of Christmas past,
there was next year, next year, always next year ...

Outside clean plate glass, snow mixed with smoke.
Christmas after Christmas we watched our city
change as girdered sepulchres replaced pure brick
and stone. While the last pie crust was lifted
from the plate, Gateway Center conquered the thrift shops
and warehouses of my mother's youth; just as,
much later, Three Rivers Stadium would rise and fall.
On winter evenings our radios played *The Messiah*
to restore us to belief and, perhaps, innocence.

The Purification

All those summers we were on the edge
of the swamp, the Great Dismal Swamp,
stretching, as it does, from Portsmouth
south past Old Trap, embracing mystery hamlets
—Burnt Mills, Shiloh, Moyock— and people
known only to those massive freighters
sliding through the canal when rough doings
battered the Outer Banks.
Those were days of darkness and beauty,
the darkness sometimes illuminated
as if there had been another world,
another river draining this land
into Albemarle Sound: a world
I never saw. I now believe there are places
where the great dream can be understood
—certainly not Washington, nor even
Richmond—places like Pungo,
listening to the ball game, Tidewater
carrying a two run lead into
the top of the eighth.
On the brink of old age, I like to think
of that swamp, the way it removed
poisons from the rain, from our polluted air,
the way it purified dark water, releasing
it into light the September Eisenhower sent
the troops into Little Rock.

Cape Henry & Cape Charles

Some thirteen miles separate two Virginia capes
that stand guard over the old estuary
of the Susquehanna River where it ran
before the glaciers melted and our oceans rose
flooding broad river valleys with salt water.
Sand, pines, and brackish backwaters—
every feature tempest-carved, every dune
bound by grasses or flung loose
into the arms of inland trees as beach
and inlet reshape into a new, stark beauty.

Where Capt. John Smith made landfall in 1607,
only the chop and swell of the restless Atlantic,
the white turbulence at the raw edge of this
shipwreck coast, meets the human eye.
So much blood spilt for what?—tobacco, slavery,
and the Church of England? The Piedmont stripped
clean to the Blue Ridge, Indians vanquished,
flood planes polluted. Still, Cape Henry broods
as always, a fragile graveyard of lost hopes
flayed by each passing squall.

Poison Ivy

The red barn still stands beside
a road so stony no grader
has ever kept it smooth. The wall
that catches the sun is covered
in poison ivy clean to the eaves.
Even on the hottest afternoons
the ivy keeps its lush, rich green.

The once-scarlet paint has weathered,
but come autumn a jubilation
of flaming ivy lights up every
fleeting day that we may adore
and begin to imagine
a beauty beyond our own human
creations, our own finite lives.

June Thunder

Today thunder came out of the west.
It came over the cliff and down the valley
sending birds into the forest's shelter.

It was like this in far western Virginia:
dark clouds, lightning, but no rain,
an early summer drought

still unbroken. We were trying to make
Middlesboro and the Gap for supper,
vast clouds covering the Cumberland Mountains;

a terrain Generals Bragg and Burnside
marched through not a hundred years before,
still terrible in its beauty.

We each make our own journey.
Sometimes thunder in the mountains
is more than thunder, rain striking

the pawpaw leaves where a river broadens,
the children dashing out barefoot
a new day in their upturned palms.

Ghost Fires

Bluefield, West Virginia. A town not half the size
it was in my youth, still clinging to the base
of its mountain. Throughout the valley to the southeast,
in a certain light, at a certain time of day,
the fields of grain can appear blue—
can *be* blue—like a purity arising
from the very earth.

The Deahls grew oats and timothy for feed,
corn for humans, much to the north,
up near the Pennsylvania line,
but their fields never possessed that blue sheen
on the long, bending leaves.

Sometimes an old mine will burn for decades,
pale flames licking up from crevices,
turning leftover coal into ghost fires in pastures
and waste lands all along the Allegheny Range.
In the small hours the coal becomes all colours,
becomes the violet of sunset, the blue of fields of grain
in the long, green evenings where the southland
rises into mountains.

On nights of the new moon the old coal
provides the only light marking the black dreams
of the hollow, the dreams we wake to
in night's blue silence.

Ulysses

The universe is made of stories,
not of atoms.
—Muriel Rukeyser

When Ulysses grew frail he lived in Parsons,
on the second floor of a rest home.
On all sides Monongahela National Forest
swept over ridge after ridge of West Virginia.
Blackgum, stave oak, sourwood
flamed up in mixed stands:
a searing red and orange as the frost
came heavy to the hill country.

King of Ithaca, mighty warrior
of Trojan battles, how then is this sick,
old man Ulysses? Ah, grandfather,
your depleted bones and black lungs
have betrayed you into the hands
of nurses, of doctors too young, perhaps,
to understand a miner's pride.

But in your green season, you rose in the dark
to light fire where fire had died,
calling flames from roses of death
to warm the home, heat water for washing.
A wife and eight children up near Chestnut Ridge.

Then out into autumn paths emblazoned
by scarlet hands of sourwood, burning lobes
of blackgum, from every tree a song of birds
heading south ...

Finally, to end alone in Parsons wondering
whose lungs you can use to breathe,
whose throat to sing.

Switzerland Of America, Gauley Bridge

Wooden storefronts line the west bank of the Gauley River
where Scrabble Creek runs in; place where men threw across
a bridge that gave the village its name, place where men laboured
and died. A hotel for commercial travellers, a speakeasy
down the street; all the expected items: post office, bank,
not that folks had money for banking after '29,
a train station. And, of course, the graveyard.
Throughout Appalachia, miners die of black lung;
here seven hundred died from white lung, crystal lung,
the sparkle of silica. Sycamores reclaim deserted strip mines;
what tree will reclaim this?

Switzerland of America — morning mist rising to unveil
a new world, to reveal an unsullied world, as things might
have looked on the day following Creation. Fresh dew
and riversong; bottomlands burst joyous with mating birds,
wildflowers emerge into light as flowing waters speak.
The purple-brown of pawpaw blossoms so like
the flowering wild ginger or the rich colour of a living heart.
And rising above all else, purple-blue ridges
so near to Heaven, yet so near that mountain
where seven decades past, Union Carbide drove a tunnel
straight through Hell.

The Mountain Fern

Where the woodshed blocks the sun
ferns grow among kindling and
old beams. No fires have been built
in the parlour stove for four
decades, so these ferns flourish
undisturbed in their moist shade.

Returning to the homestead
I seek an innocence that
can never have existed
in such a remote coal camp
amid sixty-hour weeks,
the daily struggle for bread.

Perhaps we need to believe,
against all odds, in a life
unblemished and pure to hold
us sane; like listening to
the *Goldberg Variations*
in the desolate hours

or discovering in these
wild mountain ferns a beauty
that can only be an act
of simple grace, redeeming
in its soft, green sweep a land
once scarred to its blue-grey shale.

Medix Run

In memoriam: Magdaline Florence Muller Beltz,
1870–1957

In the back country, two dozen miles beyond Du Bois,
lay Medix Run, abandoned, then forgotten
by the swelling tides of empire. So remote
from any seat of power, Elk County was known
to city folk only for its wolves and winter.
No place of purchase for Lowell's Luciferian children;
here the snake in the woodpile was simply that,
a reptile after rodents, not our souls.

Mere days after I turned twelve, grand-aunt Maggie died—
so birthday slid into funeral like an early
December snow. That year, the first atomic power plant
opened at Shippingport, not that anyone noticed;
but we all noticed Sputnik that autumn, cleaving cold skies
like a wizard's conjuring sign. With our telescopes
we were open-eyed as Jack-o'-lanterns standing
in a field. We thought time'd jumped a century in a day.

Poor aunt Maggie, no Yorkshire Puritan she, but carved
of stout Germanic stock, the kind that fled
their Teutonic princes, to build up Germantown
in the shimmer of William Penn's New World dream.
She lived so far off the paved road that shadowed
Bennett Creek, I could never find her house today.
In my youth I thought it was the edge of the world,
such great forests sweeping away above her yard.

The collie roamed the woods at will. Her house was small,
each room utilized for maximum economy;
her kitchen smelled of foursquare German cookery.
How our 1950 Ford would climb the hill in low
into a glow of day-lilies pushing out into the lane!
A sturdy village of people hardened by hard work,
their features sharpened as the seasons turned.
Back then one good job could keep a family.

These days only death seems to summon us together;
I last saw her daughters, Genevieve and Florence,
at my grandmother's graveside. My one remaining
passed-down keepsake: a child's chair made in Austria
over a century past. Towns take to logging or
dry up like gourds rattling on winter's vine.
Perhaps the dream's run out of time, but on my final
visit, hollyhocks burst with beauty by her door.

The Passing Of The Light At Horseheads

In memoriam:
Brigadier-General Orman G. Charles, U.S. Army,
1908–2006

What power
Preserves what once was, if memory does not last?
—Czesław Miłosz

How little an obituary tells
about a man in his flag-draped coffin—
dates of birth and death, degrees earned,
honours, promotions, the Korean War.
A life in service to his country.

Well before the arrival of the
Chemung County Color Guard and the
Military Forces Honor Guard
I walk the streets of Horseheads,
the older part he would have known

as a boy during World War I.
A tad too far south of Seneca Lake
to draw tourists, its industries shut
or failing, the town hangs on
with old folks' homes and veterans.

Intermittent rain falls lightly as
I tread the first slate sidewalks
I've seen in over forty years
wondering where facts end and truths begin.
Perhaps only stories contain a life.

What was Horseheads like when he watched
men march off to the War to End All Wars?
What factories flourished; what did he
think of the Black Sox scandal,
that autumn when innocence died?

The frame homes still stand, gracious
and glowing, behind their sidewalk trees
and their beds of tended flowers. But it's not
the same, can never recapture
that confidence in man's stride and reach.

In the Chapel the Presbyterian pastor
reads from *Lamentations*; we all sing
"Onward, Christian Soldiers".
There is an assurance of the reward
the righteous receive in Heaven

and I pray it will be so.
But what of this life, what of
his valour lives on? The memories of a scatter
of old men about to pass away themselves?
Or some service records filed at the Pentagon?

An agèd Christian soldier, he regretted
being too frail, too long into the winter of his years,
to take up his duty against the terrorists.
I look at the photo taken the day he received
his star and our eyes meet for the last time.

At the cemetery, the rain returns.
The flag is folded. The words of gratitude
are spoken and six men who did not know him
fire their salute under dreadnaught clouds.
The sudden report rolls ever fainter through

spreading maples. The only sounds kept forever
in our hearts are rain and *Taps*.
And the order of the universe?
It remains, as do all our virtuous deeds,
the evil perishing with the final breath.

Maple Grove: a few acres set apart
from the townland in a hush of trees
as if their great trunks could restrain time,
could protect the dead, each branch shielding
those laid below from sun or life's storms.

If in the midst of life we are in death,
then in the midst of death life is spared—
in this green world every shrub
keeps its promise, every bird
soars true, its flight a flash of glory.

In the stateliness of rural America,
in the eyes of people not embittered,
compassion moves like fingers of rain
searching through a summer's leaves
for deepening roots, for the good earth.

Notes & Credits

Ink On Paper: Jackson Pollock, 1951: The sequence mentioned in my poem is known as CR811, CR828, CR827, CR815, CR816, and CR826.

Barton Street Bus: The line by Harvey Shapiro is from his poem "Tight Like That" in *National Cold Storage: New and Selected Poems*, Wesleyan University Press, 1988.

Walking In An All-day Fog At The Close Of Autumn: The excerpted two lines from "Canto LXXXI" at the beginning of my poem "Walking In An All-day Fog At The Close Of Autumn" are from THE CANTOS OF EZRA POUND, copyright © 1948 by Ezra Pound. Reprinted by permission of New Directions Publishing Corp.

Reply To Czesław Miłosz: Please see Czesław Miłosz's poem "December 1" in *Provinces*, The Ecco Press, 1991.

Reading Dickinson While Listening To Schubert's 3rd: Dickinson's poem is on page 113 of *The Selected Poems of Emily Dickinson*, The Modern Library, 2000.

On First Looking Into Allen's The New American Poetry: Please see "The Kingfishers" by Charles Olson and "Prayerwheel" by David Meltzer in *The New American Poetry*, Donald M. Allen, Editor, Grove Press, 1960. This anthology, more than any other book, launched me in the direction I have taken in poetry since 1964.

In Jean Joubert's Kitchen: The quote from Jean Joubert can be translated as: "The poem newborn of morning ..." It is taken from his poem "Écriture du vent".

Switzerland Of America, Gauley Bridge: Please see "The Book of the Dead" by Muriel Rukeyser from her book *U.S. 1*, and collected in *A Muriel Rukeyser Reader*, Jan Heller Levi, Editor, W.W. Norton, 1994.

Medix Run: Medix Run is a village on the divide that runs the length of the Appalachian Mountains. In Pennsylvania, this high ridge separates the waters that ultimately flow down the Susquehanna River to Chesapeake Bay from the waters that enter the Gulf of Mexico via the Mississippi River. The creek at my grand-aunt's home was just on the eastern side of this divide.

The Passing Of The Light At Horseheads: The excerpted two lines from "On Parting with My Wife, Janina" at the beginning of my poem "The Passing Of The Light At Horseheads" are from THE COLLECTED POEMS: 1931-1987 by CZESLAW MILOSZ. Copyright © 1988 by Czeslaw Milosz Royalties, Inc. Reprinted by permission of HarperCollins Publishers.

Acknowledgements

Almost all of the poems in this collection have been published in periodicals or anthologies. Some poems appear here in slightly different form. The author thanks the editors of the following magazines and anthologies for their support of his poetry.

Magazines

Acumen (England); *The Ambassador* (Cuba); *Appalachian Heritage* (USA); *Atlanta Review* (USA); *Blue Collar Review* (USA); *Blueline* (USA); *Cabaret Vert; Cairn: The St. Andrews Review* (USA); *California Quarterly* (USA); *Canadian Stories; Caprice* (USA); *Clackamas Literary Review* (USA); *Confrontation* (USA); *Connecticut Review* (USA); *Cyphers* (Ireland); *Dream Catcher* (England); *The Dusty Owl Quarterly; The Fourth River* (USA); *Good Times; Hammered Out; The Hollins Critic* (USA); *Home Planet News* (USA); *Icon* (USA); *The Iconoclast* (USA); *Iodine Poetry Journal* (USA); *Janus Head* (USA); *The Louisiana Review* (USA); *Mad Poets Review* (USA); *The Nashwaak Review; The New Chief Tongue; Palo Alto Review* (USA); *Pennine Platform* (England); *Philadelphia Poets* (USA); *Pittsburgh Poetry Review* (USA); *Poemata; Poetry Nottingham* (England); *Potomac Review* (USA); *The Prairie Journal of Canadian Literature; Quercus Review* (USA); *The South Carolina Review* (USA); *Story-Quilt; Talking River* (USA); *The Texas Review* (USA); *Tower Poetry; Voices Israel* (Israel); *War, Literature & the Arts* (USA); *William & Mary Review* (USA); and *Windsor Review.*

Anthologies

Several of these poems have also been included in anthologies. The author thanks the editors and publishers of the following books for selecting his poetry:

And Left a Place to Stand On: Poems and Essays on Al Purdy (Brighton: Hidden Brook Press, 2009): The Jack Pine and North Of The Great Lakes

Cherish Our Heritage (London: HMS Press, 2004): Smith's Knoll

Gandhi Peace Festival (Hamilton: McMaster University, Centre for Peace Studies, 2005 & 2006 editions): Cardinal; Saturday Morning With Sulak; and Siblings

Henry's Creature: Poems and Stories on the automobile (Windsor: Black Moss Press, 2000): Going Off The Road Near Bishops Mills

Myth Weavers: Canadian Myths and Legends (Waterdown: Serengeti Press, 2007): Listening To The Women Of The Wind

October (Kitchener: Poetry and Good Cheer Press, 2005): Late October At Rockwood

Spirit Valley Rambles (Rockwood: privately published by Katherine L. Gordon, 2006): Walking To The Eramosa During The Time Of Harvest

An Unfinished War: War of 1812 Poetry & Prose (Windsor: Black Moss Press, 2012): Smith's Knoll

Winter Solitudes (Kitchener: Poetry and Good Cheer Press, 2006): Quilts

Virtual Anthologies

Poets Against the War (first volume, 2003): Cardinal

Poets Against the War (second volume, 2003): Siblings

Books & Chapbooks

Landscapes (Metulla, Israel: Cyclamens and Swords Publishing, 2016): The Jack Pine; Late October At Rockwood; Listening To The Women Of The Wind; and North Of The Great Lakes

Love Where Our Nights Are Long (Mt. Pleasant: Laurel Reed Books, 2008): Love Where Our Nights Are Long

North Point (Toronto: Lyricalmyrical, 2012): The Jack Pine

Two Paths Through The Seasons (Metulla, Israel: Cyclamens and Swords Publishing, 2014): Silence In The Fields Of Autumn

The poems in this collection, whatever their merits, greatly benefited from the editorial advice of Ronnie R. Brown, Norma West Linder, Carol Malyon, Michael Wurster, and, most especially, Gilda L. Mekler. I owe them a great debt for improvements of selection, phrase, and construction.

Previous Awards

"Autumn Barns" won the Monica Ladell Award in 2013.

"Medix Run" (in the present collection) won the Amy Tritsch Needle Award (3rd prize) in 2012.

When Rivers Speak (2001) won the Ramada Plaza Hotel Award.

Tasting The Winter Grapes (1995) won the Award of Excellence from the Hamilton & Region Arts Council.

A poem in his haiku collection, *Blue Ridge* (1985), won the Mainichi Award (Tokyo, Japan).

Publications List

To Be With a Woman (Lummox Press, 2016)
Landscapes (Cyclamens and Swords, 2016)
Unbroken Lines (Lummox Press, 2015)
Two Paths Through The Seasons (Cyclamens and Swords, 2014)
North Point (Lyricalmyrical, 2012)
Rooms The Wind Makes (Guernica Editions, 2012)
North Of Belleville (Hidden Brook Press, 2012)
Opening The Stone Heart (Aeolus House, 2010)
No Star Is Lost (Lyricalmyrical, 2009)
Love Where Our Nights Are Long (Laurel Reed Books, 2008)
If Ever Two Were One (Aeolus House, 2008)
The River's Stone Roots: Two dozen poems by Tu Fu (Serengeti Press, 2005)
When Rivers Speak (Unfinished Monument Press, 2001)
Blackbirds (Unfinished Monument Press, 1999)
Under The Watchful Eye (Broken Jaw Press, 1995)
Tasting The Winter Grapes (Envoi Poets Publications, 1995)
Even This Land Was Born Of Light (Moonstone Press, 1993)
Heartland (Envoi Poets Publications, 1993)
Geschriebene Bilder (M+N Boesche Verlag, Berlin, 1990)
A Stand Of Jackpine (Unfinished Monument Press, 1987)
Into This Dark Earth (Unfinished Monument Press, 1985)
Blue Ridge (Aureole Point Press, 1985)
No Cold Ash (Sono Nis Press, 1984)
Steel Valley (Aureole Point Press, 1984)
In The Lost Horn's Call (Aureole Point Press, 1982)
Real Poetry (Unfinished Monument Press, 1981)

About the Author

JAMES DEAHL was born in Pittsburgh in 1945, and grew up in that city as well as in and around the Laurel Highlands of the Appalachian Mountains. He moved to Canada in 1970 and holds Canadian citizenship. He's the author (or, in the case of Tu Fu's poetry, translator) of twenty-six literary titles. His most recent books are *To Be With A Woman*, *Landscapes* (with Katherine L. Gordon), *Unbroken Lines*, *Two Paths Through The Seasons* (with Norma West Linder), and *Rooms The Wind Makes* (Guernica Editions).

A cycle of his poems is the focus of a one-hour TV special, *Under the Watchful Eye*. Both the video and an audiotape have been reissued on CD and DVD by Silver Falls Video. In addition to his writing, he has taught creative writing and Canadian literature at the high school, college, and university levels. He no longer teaches, and for the past fifteen years has mostly been a full-time writer/editor/translator. James Deahl lives in Sarnia. He is the father of Sarah, Simone, and Shona (with whom he is translating the poetry of Émile Nelligan), and the grandfather of Rebekah.